W9-CIO-959

EXPLORING WORLD CULTURES

Peru

Ruth Bjorklund

Cavendish
Square

New York

For Neil, my guide through Lima

Published in 2017 by Cavendish Square Publishing, LLC
243 5th Avenue, Suite 136, New York, NY 10016

CPSIA Compliance Information: Batch #CS16CSQ

All websites were available and accurate when this book was sent to press.

Library of Congress Cataloging-in-Publication Data

Names: Bjorklund, Ruth, author.
Title: Peru / Ruth Bjorklund.
Description: New York : Cavendish Square Pub., 2017. | Series: Exploring world cultures | Includes index.
Identifiers: LCCN 2016003656 (print) | LCCN 2016004052 (ebook) |
ISBN 9781502618078 (pbk.) | ISBN 9781502617996 (library bound) |
ISBN 9781502617842 (6 pack) | ISBN 9781502617361 (ebook)
Subjects: LCSH: Peru--Juvenile literature.
Classification: LCC F3408.5 .B46 2017 (print) | LCC F3408.5 (ebook) |
DDC 985--dc23
LC record available at http://lccn.loc.gov/2016003656

Editorial Director: David McNamara
Editor: Kristen Susienka
Copy Editor: Rebecca Rohan
Art Director: Jeffrey Talbot
Designer: Joseph Macri
Production Assistant: Karol Szymczuk
Photo Research: J8 Media

The photographs in this book are used by permission and through the courtesy of: Nathalie Michel /The Image Bank/Getty Images, cover; Goran Bogicevic/Shutterstock.com, 5; pavalena/Shutterstock.com, 6; Rafal Cichawa/Shutterstock.com, 7; AISA/Bridgeman Images, 8; Pyty/Shutterstock.com, 9; Atosan/Shutterstock.com, 10; chelovek/iStock, 11; Glowimages/Getty Images, 12; aroas/iStock, 13; Holger Mette/iStock, 14; Mark Bowler/Alamy Stock Photo, 15; Bartosz Hadyniak/iStock, 16, 19, 24, 25; Sven Schermer/Shutterstock.com, 18; DC_Colombia/iStock, 20; Johnny Haglund/Lonely Planet Images/Getty Images, 22; Raul Sifuentes/LatinContent/Getty Images, 26; Tiago Lopes Fernandez/Shutterstock.com, 28; Foodio/Shutterstock.com.

Printed in the United States of America

Contents

There are many exciting countries in the world. Some are big, and some are small. Peru is a fun country in South America.

Since long ago, many different groups have lived in Peru. The largest group was the Inca people. The Incas built cities in the mountains. Inca armies fought other groups and built a large empire. A leader called an emperor ruled them. Later, Spanish explorers arrived. They killed many Incas.

Today, the people of Peru are called Peruvians. Nearly everyone speaks Spanish. Peruvians work hard. They also spend time with their friends and family. Peruvians enjoy music and art. Many Peruvians like the outdoors.

Peru has deserts, rain forests, mountains, and beaches. Many animals, plants, and trees live in Peru.

Some people live in small towns and villages, but most people live in cities. In both city and country, people celebrate festivals and holidays. Peruvians are very proud of their country.

Three girls wear traditional Peruvian clothing.

Geography

Peru has three parts, called regions. The Pacific Coast region is in the west. The Andes Mountain region is in the center. Animals like llamas and **vicuñas** live there. The Amazon rain forest region is in the east.

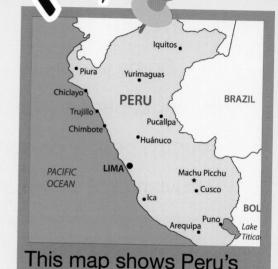

This map shows Peru's long coastline.

Monkeys, jaguars, colorful flowers and trees, and many fish and snakes live there.

Volcano Mountain

Peru's tallest mountain, Mount Huascarán, is a snow-covered volcano about 4 miles (6 kilometers) high.

Peru has many rivers and lakes. Peru also has one of the world's deepest lakes. It is called Lake Titicaca.

The tallest mountain in the Andes is covered in clouds.

In Peru, the seasons are different. It is winter in July and summer in December. It rains almost every day in winter. It can get hot in summer.

The coast has mild temperatures. The Andes Mountains are warm in the daytime and cold at night. The rain forest is warm all year.

FACT!

The world's second-longest river, the Amazon River, begins in Peru.

Ancient Peruvians called Incas farmed, fished, and raised animals. They also built stone temples and made pottery. The Incas invented many things, such as a calendar and musical instruments.

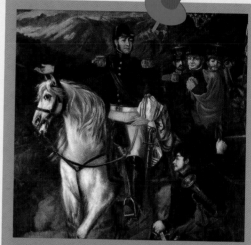

General San Martín crosses the Andes.

In 1531, a Spanish soldier named Francisco Pizarro arrived. He met the Incas and wanted to control their land. Pizarro and his soldiers defeated the Inca empire in 1533. They took over the Incas' treasures and treated people cruelly. Spain ruled Peru until a South American general named José de San Martín declared Peru independent in 1821.

Machu Picchu

Machu Picchu is an Incan city in the Andes Mountains. There are ruins of temples, forts, palaces, and a pyramid that people can visit today.

Machu Picchu is a popular tourist area.

Since then, many generals and presidents have ruled Peru. At times, Peru has gone to war with its neighbors. Today, Peru has a president.

FACT!

During World War II, Peruvians collected bark from a special tree in the rain forest to make medicine for soldiers.

VOTE ✓

Peru's official name is the Republic of Peru. Lawmakers wrote a **constitution** in 1993. It divided the government into three branches: executive, legislative, and judicial.

The president leads the executive branch. There are two vice presidents and a group of fifteen council ministers, including one prime

FACT!

Francisco Pizarro moved Peru's capital from the Incan city of Cuzco to the coastal city of Lima, so shipments of gold to Spain would be easier.

The Governor's Palace in Lima

minister. No law can be passed without the Council of Ministers' approval.

The legislative branch has 120 members. It is their job to make laws. The judicial branch is led by a supreme court. There are 25 regional courts and many city courts.

The Flag

Peru's flag is red and white. Some of the symbols on the flag are: gold coins; the tree used to make medicine; and the vicuña, a rare animal that stands for freedom and national pride.

The Peruvian flag was officially adopted in 1824.

The Economy

Peru's **economy** has had many problems, but it is better now. Most Peruvians live in cities. Some people work as teachers, firefighters, maids, construction workers, and

Many farmers plant their crops on hillsides.

people who fix cars. People also have jobs in banking, health care, business, and law. In the country, people farm, mine, or raise animals.

Mining is important to Peru's economy. Peru sells copper, silver, and gold to other countries. Other products sent to other countries are cars, clothing, and items made from the soft wool of alpacas and vicuñas.

Visiting Peru

Tourism is the third-largest industry in Peru. Every year, people from around the world visit Machu Picchu, the Andes Mountains, and the Amazon rain forest.

Farmers produce coffee, cotton, sugarcane, rice, potatoes, corn, wheat, and fruit. They also raise chickens and cows. Fishermen catch fish in the ocean and rivers.

Soles banknotes

FACT!

Peruvian money is called *sol,* meaning "sun." One sol equals about thirty US cents.

The Environment

Most Peruvians live in big cities near the ocean. Every day, cars, trucks, and factories dirty the air, the rivers, and the ocean. These activities are bad for the **environment**.

Lima has more dirty air than other South American cities.

Copper, gold, and silver mines in the Andes Mountains use harmful chemicals. The chemicals poison the water. Many fish die because the water they live in is poisoned.

Peru's rain forest is home to many plants and animals. Loggers cut down rain-forest trees. This takes away many animals' homes. Logging, hunting, and stealing animals hurt Peru's wildlife population.

An Animal in Danger

The yellow-tailed woolly monkey is an animal that lives only in the Peruvian Andes. Mining and logging are destroying its home.

The yellow-tailed woolly monkey is very rare.

Peru is making laws to care for the land. It has special areas that protect plants and animals. Mining, logging, and other harmful activities are not allowed there.

Rain-forest trees clean dirty air in the Earth's atmosphere and make oxygen.

The People Today

Many people in Peru are related to ancient Peruvians. Today, there are more than one hundred Native groups, or tribes, in Peru. The largest are the Quechua and Aymara tribes. Many

A Native couple enjoys an afternoon walk.

Quechua and Aymara people are farmers and herders. The Quechua live in the Andes Mountains.

FACT!

Many Peruvians in the rain forest have never seen anyone from outside their village.

16

The Crowded Andes

More people live in the Andes than in any other mountain range in the world.

The Aymara live on the desert **highlands**. There are tribes that live in the rain forest, too.

When Europeans arrived, many married Native people. Today about one-third of Peruvians are a mix of Native and European groups. Other Peruvians came from China, Japan, and Africa.

All people in Peru have their own celebrations and customs. Many families in Peru enjoy seeing their friends and family and celebrating with them.

17

Lifestyle

Family life is important to Peruvians. In cities, parents and children often live near grandparents, aunts, uncles, and cousins. After parents come home from work and children come home from school, many visit parks or take walks together.

Lima's parks and waterfront paths are popular.

 FACT!

More than one-quarter of all Peruvians live in Lima, the country's capital city.

People of the Andes

Many Peruvians in the Andes wear colorful, **traditional** clothes and hats.

Families in the country all work together. Children have jobs, such as planting potatoes. The Aymara people farm in the desert. It is hard work because the soil is not good. Farmers

These women are dressed in traditional clothes.

in the Andes grow food on steep hillsides. Today, some farmers leave to find jobs in cities.

The people of the rain forest make their own clothes and hunt and grow their food. They build their houses from leaves and grass. There are almost no roads. People travel on foot or by boat.

The Native people of Peru believed there were spirits inside all living things, the sky, and the earth. The Incas **worshipped** gods and goddesses. The sun god was

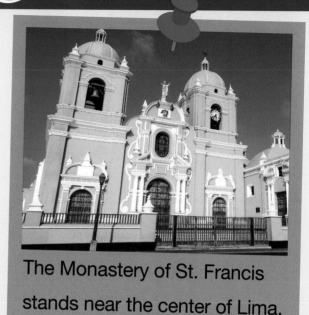

The Monastery of St. Francis stands near the center of Lima.

their most important god. He was married to the goddess of the moon. The people built many temples, called *huacas*, to celebrate the gods.

FACT!

The name of the Inca goddess Pachamama means "Mother Earth." Farmers prayed to her for a good harvest.

When the Spanish explorers arrived, they brought a new religion called Catholicism. They taught the Natives about Catholic beliefs and built many churches on top of the huacas. They believed the Native people would accept the Catholic faith if Catholic churches and Native temples were built in the same place.

Today, most Peruvians are Catholic. Some other Peruvians are Protestant, Mormon, Buddhist, and Muslim.

The Oldest Church in Peru

The oldest Catholic Church in Peru was built in 1535.

Language

There are more than ninety different languages spoken in Peru. Most Peruvians speak Spanish. Some Native people speak only Quechua or Aymara.

A boy listens in geography class.

All three languages are official languages of Peru. Some languages are very old. People living in the Amazon rain forest and the Andes Mountains speak old languages.

There are many people who moved to Peru from other countries. They speak the language of their home country. Some Peruvians speak Chinese, Japanese, German, Italian, or Arabic.

After the Incas conquered the Quechua tribe, they chose Quechua as their language. The first Spanish explorers learned Quechua, too.

Most newspapers, TV channels, and radio stations are in Spanish. Children learn Spanish in schools. The government uses Spanish. Many Peruvians want others to learn Native languages, too.

Lima's Chinatown

The largest Chinatown in South America is in Lima. People call the neighborhood by its Spanish name, Barrio Chino.

Arts and Festivals

Peruvians are very artistic. They make colorful fabric and pottery. Ancient Incas used gold and silver to decorate their belongings. Today, many Peruvian jewelers copy Inca designs.

A weaver makes cloth using a tool called a loom.

Many buildings in Peru are beautiful. Visitors are amazed when they see the Inca temples and palaces at Machu Picchu. Cities have many Spanish-style buildings.

Peruvians celebrate holidays all year. Some are religious holidays, such as Easter and

In February, Peruvians celebrate Carnival. Along with singing and dancing, people plant big trees and put presents under them.

Christmas. Others are native Peruvian holidays, such as the first day of summer.

A musician plays a wooden flute.

Peruvians enjoy music and dance. The Incas invented the flute and the panpipe. A panpipe is made of wooden tubes with small holes. The tubes are tied together. Musicians blow across the tubes to make sounds.

FACT!

The Scissor Dance is popular at Peru's festivals. Dancers move quickly and make big leaps and turns.

Fun and Play

Peruvians like to have fun. In cities, the parks are full every day with families and friends enjoying a picnic or a game of *fútbol* (soccer). People in cities also enjoy movies, concerts,

Fans cheer for Peru's national soccer team.

and eating in restaurants. Lima has a large zoo, and many cities have interesting museums.

FACT!

In the evening, people gather to chat with their friends in the town square, which is called a *zocalo*.

Children play many traditional South American games. They like to play clapping games, marbles, and circle games with lots of jumping and chanting. Many Peruvians enjoy boating, swimming, and hiking.

Peruvians are wild about fútbol. The national team has competed in several World Cup soccer matches.

Nicknames

Two nicknames for Peru's national futbol team are Los Incas and La Blanquirroja. La Blanquirroja means "The Red and White" and refers to the colors of Peru's flag.

Food

People eat different foods in different areas of Peru. In the Andes Mountains, people eat potatoes, quinoa, and meat, such as pork and llama.

Many small farms raise at least one or two animals.

In the rain forest, people enjoy fruits, such as mangoes and bananas. People eat bananas with almost every meal. They eat them fried, grilled, mashed, or raw. They eat a lot of fish, too.

FACT!

One national dish is called *cuy*. It is guinea pig.

People in cities eat all types of foods. Lima is famous for its restaurants and food. People eat meat, fish, fruits, and vegetables. Cooks use spices from

Ceviche is salty, sour, and a little bit sweet.

many countries in their dishes. The most famous food is called *ceviche* (se-VEECH-ay). It is made from raw fish, lemons or limes, onions, and spices.

Peru's Potatoes

The Incas grew potatoes more than eight thousand years ago. When explorers met the Inca, they learned about potatoes. They brought potato seeds back to Europe in 1589.

29

Glossary

ancient Very old or long ago.

constitution A document that describes a country's laws.

economy A country's system of making and selling goods and services.

environment The area that surrounds where a person, animal, or plant lives.

highlands Hilly areas of land.

traditional Beliefs or customs handed down from one generation to the next.

vicuña A wild animal of the Andes related to camels and llamas.

worship To pay honor or respect to a divine being or a supernatural power.

Find Out More

Books

Hinman, Bonnie. *We Visit Peru*. Hockessin, DE:
Mitchell Lane Publishers, 2010.

Richardson, Gillian. *Machu Picchu*. New York:
Weigl Publishers, 2013.

Websites

Inca Empire for Kids

incas.mrdonn.org

Time for Kids: Peru

www.timeforkids.com/destination/peru

Video

NeoK12 Educational Videos and Games

www.neok12.com/Countries-States.htm (Select
Peru from list.)

Learn more about Peru here.

Index

About the Author

Ruth Bjorklund has written many books for young people. She lives on an island near Seattle, Washington. In 2015, she and her son visited Peru. They went to the Andes, Lima, and the rain forest.